SHOT SPOTS

BUCKET LIST BOOK

FOR PHOTOGRAPHERS:
Keep Track of Your Top 40 Shot Spots!

📷 Barbara Jean

Minneapolis, MN

Published by Sun Lion Publications in 2015
First Printing, First Edition

Design & writing ©2015 by Barbara Jean
Cover background image by Stux

All rights reserved. No part of this book may be reproduced or transmitted in any form or by any means, including but not limited to information storage and retrieval systems, electronic, mechanical, photocopy, recording, etc. without written permission from the copyright holder.

ISBN # 978-0-9967599-0-8

Dedication

This book is dedicated to all those in pursuit of that next awesome shot.

Also to my family, who I drive a little crazy now and then with my relentless picture taking!

How to use this book

The purpose of this book is to keep all of your various bucket list shot spot ideas organized in one, easy-to-find place. Here are some guidelines so you can make the most out of using this book:

1. Use the fill-in-the-blank Table of Contents to keep track of where you put each shot spot. This will make it easy for you to find those spots later.

2. The first line in each section is to write in your shot spot. It could be a place that you heard about in a photography group, read in a magazine, heard about from a friend, or viewed on Facebook.

3. Most ideas we get are inspired from something we see or hear. Paying attention to the details may get you some new shot spots for your list.

4. There are plenty of topic headings to fill in for each spot. Just fill in the lines that apply to each particular shot spot - you may or may not have the info for all of them.

5. "Shot spot concept" is the place to flesh out the shot spot idea further, and down below is a box for any drawings you may need to make.

6. There are lines to keep track of location info, contact info, planning and resources, gear, lighting, permissions, fees, and finally any thoughts or impressions after you have been there.

7. Enjoy crossing shot spots off your photography bucket list!

Table of Contents

Fill in these page # blanks with each shot spot for quick reference!

Page	
9	___
13	___
17	___
21	___
25	___
29	___
33	___
37	___
41	___
45	___
49	___
53	___
57	___
61	___
65	___
69	___
73	___
77	___
81	___
85	___
89	___
93	___
97	___

Table of Contents, continued

Fill in these page # blanks with each shot spot for quick reference!

101 _____
105 _____
109 _____
113 _____
117 _____
121 _____
125 _____
129 _____
133 _____
137 _____
141 _____
145 _____
149 _____
153 _____
157 _____
161 _____
165 _____
169 Shot Spot Website Resource

Shot Spot: _____

Date: _____

Distance: _____

Coordinates: _____

Address:
_____
_____

Email: _____

Website: _____

Time of Day: _____

Lighting (sunlight, flash, diffused light, etc.):
_____
_____

Gear List:
_____
_____
_____
_____

Fee? Yes or No/Amount$: _____

Need Permission? Yes or No/Notes:
_____
_____
_____
_____

Shot Spot Concept (What, how, etc.):

_____
_____
_____
_____
_____
_____
_____
_____
_____
_____
_____
_____
_____

Sketch Area:

"Photography takes an instant out of time, altering life by holding it still." -Dorothea Lange

Tips from others who have been there (Google, friends, where to stay, where to eat):
_____
_____
_____
_____
_____
_____
_____

Planning/Resources (Ex: social media pages, books to read, how many days, best month to go, book hotel, etc): _____
_____
_____
_____
_____
_____
_____
_____
_____

Mission Accomplished! Date: _____

Fill out any thoughts here after you hit the spot (Ex: overall impression, how many photos you took, what you would do differently next time, memory to remember the trip by, best/worst thing that happened, etc.):

_____
_____
_____
_____
_____
_____
_____
_____
_____
_____
_____
_____
_____
_____
_____
_____
_____
_____
_____
_____

Shot Spot: _____

Date: _____

Distance: _____

Coordinates: _____

Address:
_____
_____

Email: _____

Website: _____

Time of Day: _____

Lighting (sunlight, flash, diffused light, etc.):
_____
_____

Gear List:
_____
_____
_____
_____

Fee? Yes or No/Amount$: _____

Need Permission? Yes or No/Notes:
_____
_____
_____
_____

Shot Spot Concept (What, how, etc.):

_____
_____
_____
_____
_____
_____
_____
_____
_____
_____
_____
_____
_____

Sketch Area:

Tips from others who have been there (Google, friends):

_____
_____
_____
_____
_____
_____
_____
_____

Planning/Resources (Ex: social media pages, books to read, how many days, best month to go, book hotel, etc):

_____
_____
_____
_____
_____
_____
_____
_____
_____
_____
_____
_____

Mission Accomplished! Date: _____

Fill out any thoughts here after you hit the spot (Ex: overall impression, how many photos you took, what you would do differently next time, memory to remember the trip by, best/worst thing that happened, etc.):

_____
_____
_____
_____
_____
_____
_____
_____
_____
_____
_____
_____
_____
_____
_____
_____
_____
_____
_____
_____

Shot Spot: _____

Date: _____

Distance: _____

Coordinates: _____

Address:
_____
_____

Email: _____

Website: _____

Time of Day: _____

Lighting (sunlight, flash, diffused light, etc.):
_____
_____

Gear List:
_____
_____
_____
_____

Fee? Yes or No/Amount$: _____

Need Permission? Yes or No/Notes:
_____
_____
_____

Shot Spot Concept (What, how, etc.):

_____
_____
_____
_____
_____
_____
_____
_____
_____
_____
_____
_____

Sketch Area:

Tips from others who have been there (Google, friends):

_____
_____
_____
_____
_____
_____
_____
_____

Planning/Resources (Ex: social media pages, books to read, how many days, best month to go, book hotel, etc):

_____
_____
_____
_____
_____
_____
_____
_____
_____
_____
_____
_____

Mission Accomplished!   Date: _____

Fill out any thoughts here after you hit the spot (Ex: overall impression, how many photos you took, what you would do differently next time, memory to remember the trip by, best/worst thing that happened, etc.):

_____
_____
_____
_____
_____
_____
_____
_____
_____
_____
_____
_____
_____
_____
_____
_____
_____
_____
_____
_____
_____

Shot Spot: _____

Date: _____

Distance: _____

Coordinates: _____

Address:
_____
_____

Email: _____

Website: _____

Time of Day: _____

Lighting (sunlight, flash, diffused light, etc.):
_____
_____

Gear List:
_____
_____
_____
_____

Fee? Yes or No/Amount$: _____

Need Permission? Yes or No/Notes:
_____
_____
_____
_____

Shot Spot Concept (What, how, etc.):

_____
_____
_____
_____
_____
_____
_____
_____
_____
_____
_____
_____
_____

Sketch Area:

Tips from others who have been there (Google, friends):

_____
_____
_____
_____
_____
_____
_____
_____

Planning/Resources (Ex: social media pages, books to read, how many days, best month to go, book hotel, etc):

_____
_____
_____
_____
_____
_____
_____
_____
_____
_____
_____

Mission Accomplished! Date: _____

Fill out any thoughts here after you hit the spot (Ex: overall impression, how many photos you took, what you would do differently next time, memory to remember the trip by, best/worst thing that happened, etc.):

_____
_____
_____
_____
_____
_____
_____
_____
_____
_____
_____
_____
_____
_____
_____
_____
_____
_____
_____
_____

Shot Spot: _____

Date: _____

Distance: _____

Coordinates: _____

Address:
_____
_____

Email: _____

Website: _____

Time of Day: _____

Lighting (sunlight, flash, diffused light, etc.):
_____
_____

Gear List:
_____
_____
_____
_____

Fee? Yes or No/Amount$: _____

Need Permission? Yes or No/Notes:
_____
_____
_____
_____

Shot Spot Concept (What, how, etc.):

Sketch Area:

> *"You can't wait for inspiration.*
> *You have to go after it with a club."*
> —Jack London

Tips from others who have been there (Google, friends, where to stay, where to eat):

_____
_____
_____
_____
_____
_____
_____
_____

Planning/Resources (Ex: social media pages, books to read, how many days, best month to go, book hotel, etc): _____

_____
_____
_____
_____
_____
_____
_____
_____
_____

Mission Accomplished! Date: _____

Fill out any thoughts here after you hit the spot (Ex: overall impression, how many photos you took, what you would do differently next time, memory to remember the trip by, best/worst thing that happened, etc.):

_____
_____
_____
_____
_____
_____
_____
_____
_____
_____
_____
_____
_____
_____
_____
_____
_____
_____
_____

Shot Spot: _____

Date: _____

Distance: _____

Coordinates: _____

Address:
_____
_____

Email: _____

Website: _____

Time of Day: _____

Lighting (sunlight, flash, diffused light, etc.):
_____
_____

Gear List:
_____
_____
_____
_____

Fee? Yes or No/Amount$: _____

Need Permission? Yes or No/Notes:
_____
_____
_____
_____

Shot Spot Concept (What, how, etc.):

_____
_____
_____
_____
_____
_____
_____
_____
_____
_____
_____
_____
_____

Sketch Area:

Tips from others who have been there (Google, friends):

_____
_____
_____
_____
_____
_____
_____
_____

Planning/Resources (Ex: social media pages, books to read, how many days, best month to go, book hotel, etc):

_____
_____
_____
_____
_____
_____
_____
_____
_____
_____
_____
_____

Mission Accomplished! Date: _____

Fill out any thoughts here after you hit the spot (Ex: overall impression, how many photos you took, what you would do differently next time, memory to remember the trip by, best/worst thing that happened, etc.):

_____
_____
_____
_____
_____
_____
_____
_____
_____
_____
_____
_____
_____
_____
_____
_____
_____
_____
_____
_____
_____

Shot Spot: _____

Date: _____

Distance: _____

Coordinates: _____

Address:

_____

_____

Email: _____

Website: _____

Time of Day: _____

Lighting (sunlight, flash, diffused light, etc.):

_____

_____

Gear List:

_____

_____

_____

_____

Fee? Yes or No/Amount$: _____

Need Permission? Yes or No/Notes:

_____

_____

_____

Shot Spot Concept (What, how, etc.):

_____
_____
_____
_____
_____
_____
_____
_____
_____
_____
_____
_____
_____

Sketch Area:

Tips from others who have been there (Google, friends):

_____
_____
_____
_____
_____
_____
_____
_____

Planning/Resources (Ex: social media pages, books to read, how many days, best month to go, book hotel, etc):

_____
_____
_____
_____
_____
_____
_____
_____
_____
_____
_____
_____

Mission Accomplished! Date: _____

Fill out any thoughts here after you hit the spot (Ex: overall impression, how many photos you took, what you would do differently next time, memory to remember the trip by, best/worst thing that happened, etc.):

_____
_____
_____
_____
_____
_____
_____
_____
_____
_____
_____
_____
_____
_____
_____
_____
_____
_____
_____
_____

Shot Spot: _____

Date: _____

Distance: _____

Coordinates: _____

Address:

_____

_____

Email: _____

Website: _____

Time of Day: _____

Lighting (sunlight, flash, diffused light, etc.):

_____

_____

Gear List:

_____

_____

_____

_____

Fee? Yes or No/Amount$: _____

Need Permission? Yes or No/Notes:

_____

_____

_____

_____

Shot Spot Concept (What, how, etc.):

Sketch Area:

Tips from others who have been there (Google, friends):

_____
_____
_____
_____
_____
_____
_____
_____
_____

Planning/Resources (Ex: social media pages, books to read, how many days, best month to go, book hotel, etc):

_____
_____
_____
_____
_____
_____
_____
_____
_____
_____
_____
_____
_____
_____

Mission Accomplished!   Date: _____

Fill out any thoughts here after you hit the spot (Ex: overall impression, how many photos you took, what you would do differently next time, memory to remember the trip by, best/worst thing that happened, etc.):

_____
_____
_____
_____
_____
_____
_____
_____
_____
_____
_____
_____
_____
_____
_____
_____
_____
_____
_____
_____
_____

Shot Spot: _____

Date: _____

Distance: _____

Coordinates: _____

Address:
_____
_____

Email: _____

Website: _____

Time of Day: _____

Lighting (sunlight, flash, diffused light, etc.):
_____
_____

Gear List:
_____
_____
_____
_____

Fee? Yes or No/Amount$: _____

Need Permission? Yes or No/Notes:
_____
_____
_____
_____

Shot Spot Concept (What, how, etc.):

Sketch Area:

"Photography helps people to see."
-Berenice Abbott

Tips from others who have been there (Google, friends, where to stay, where to eat):

_____
_____
_____
_____
_____
_____
_____

Planning/Resources (Ex: social media pages, books to read, how many days, best month to go, book hotel, etc): _____

_____
_____
_____
_____
_____
_____
_____
_____

Mission Accomplished! Date: _____

Fill out any thoughts here after you hit the spot (Ex: overall impression, how many photos you took, what you would do differently next time, memory to remember the trip by, best/worst thing that happened, etc.):

_____
_____
_____
_____
_____
_____
_____
_____
_____
_____
_____
_____
_____
_____
_____
_____
_____
_____
_____
_____

Shot Spot: _____

Date: _____

Distance: _____

Coordinates: _____

Address:
_____
_____

Email: _____

Website: _____

Time of Day: _____

Lighting (sunlight, flash, diffused light, etc.):
_____
_____

Gear List:
_____
_____
_____
_____

Fee? Yes or No/Amount$: _____

Need Permission? Yes or No/Notes:
_____
_____
_____
_____

Shot Spot Concept (What, how, etc.):

Sketch Area:

Tips from others who have been there (Google, friends):

_____
_____
_____
_____
_____
_____
_____
_____

Planning/Resources (Ex: social media pages, books to read, how many days, best month to go, book hotel, etc):

_____
_____
_____
_____
_____
_____
_____
_____
_____
_____
_____
_____
_____

Mission Accomplished!   Date: _____

Fill out any thoughts here after you hit the spot (Ex: overall impression, how many photos you took, what you would do differently next time, memory to remember the trip by, best/worst thing that happened, etc.):

_____
_____
_____
_____
_____
_____
_____
_____
_____
_____
_____
_____
_____
_____
_____
_____
_____
_____
_____
_____
_____
_____

Shot Spot: _____

Date: _____

Distance: _____

Coordinates: _____

Address:
_____
_____

Email: _____

Website: _____

Time of Day: _____

Lighting (sunlight, flash, diffused light, etc.):
_____
_____

Gear List:
_____
_____
_____
_____

Fee? Yes or No/Amount$: _____

Need Permission? Yes or No/Notes:
_____
_____
_____
_____

Shot Spot Concept (What, how, etc.):

_____
_____
_____
_____
_____
_____
_____
_____
_____
_____
_____
_____

Sketch Area:

Tips from others who have been there (Google, friends):

_____
_____
_____
_____
_____
_____
_____
_____

Planning/Resources (Ex: social media pages, books to read, how many days, best month to go, book hotel, etc):

_____
_____
_____
_____
_____
_____
_____
_____
_____
_____
_____

Mission Accomplished! Date: _____

Fill out any thoughts here after you hit the spot (Ex: overall impression, how many photos you took, what you would do differently next time, memory to remember the trip by, best/worst thing that happened, etc.):

_____
_____
_____
_____
_____
_____
_____
_____
_____
_____
_____
_____
_____
_____
_____
_____
_____
_____
_____
_____
_____

Shot Spot: _____

Date: _____

Distance: _____

Coordinates: _____

Address:
_____
_____

Email: _____

Website: _____

Time of Day: _____

Lighting (sunlight, flash, diffused light, etc.):
_____
_____

Gear List:
_____
_____
_____
_____

Fee? Yes or No/Amount$: _____

Need Permission? Yes or No/Notes:
_____
_____
_____
_____

Shot Spot Concept (What, how, etc.):

_____
_____
_____
_____
_____
_____
_____
_____
_____
_____
_____
_____
_____

Sketch Area:

Tips from others who have been there (Google, friends):

_____
_____
_____
_____
_____
_____
_____
_____

Planning/Resources (Ex: social media pages, books to read, how many days, best month to go, book hotel, etc):

_____
_____
_____
_____
_____
_____
_____
_____
_____
_____
_____
_____
_____

Mission Accomplished! Date: _____

Fill out any thoughts here after you hit the spot (Ex: overall impression, how many photos you took, what you would do differently next time, memory to remember the trip by, best/worst thing that happened, etc.):

_____
_____
_____
_____
_____
_____
_____
_____
_____
_____
_____
_____
_____
_____
_____
_____
_____
_____
_____
_____

Shot Spot: _____

Date: _____

Distance: _____

Coordinates: _____

Address:
_____
_____

Email: _____

Website: _____

Time of Day: _____

Lighting (sunlight, flash, diffused light, etc.):
_____
_____

Gear List:
_____
_____
_____
_____

Fee? Yes or No/Amount$: _____

Need Permission? Yes or No/Notes:
_____
_____
_____
_____

Shot Spot Concept (What, how, etc.):

Sketch Area:

"I love photography, I love food, and I love traveling, and to put those three things together would just be the ultimate dream." -Jamie Chung

Tips from others who have been there (Google, friends, where to stay, where to eat):

_____
_____
_____
_____
_____
_____
_____

Planning/Resources (Ex: social media pages, books to read, how many days, best month to go, book hotel, etc): _____

_____
_____
_____
_____
_____
_____
_____
_____

Mission Accomplished! Date: _____

Fill out any thoughts here after you hit the spot (Ex: overall impression, how many photos you took, what you would do differently next time, memory to remember the trip by, best/worst thing that happened, etc.):

_____
_____
_____
_____
_____
_____
_____
_____
_____
_____
_____
_____
_____
_____
_____
_____
_____
_____
_____

Shot Spot: _____

Date: _____

Distance: _____

Coordinates: _____

Address:
_____
_____

Email: _____

Website: _____

Time of Day: _____

Lighting (sunlight, flash, diffused light, etc.):
_____
_____

Gear List:
_____
_____
_____
_____

Fee? Yes or No/Amount$: _____

Need Permission? Yes or No/Notes:
_____
_____
_____
_____

Shot Spot Concept (What, how, etc.):

_____
_____
_____
_____
_____
_____
_____
_____
_____
_____
_____
_____
_____
_____

Sketch Area:

Tips from others who have been there (Google, friends):
_____
_____
_____
_____
_____
_____
_____
_____

Planning/Resources (Ex: social media pages, books to read, how many days, best month to go, book hotel, etc):
_____
_____
_____
_____
_____
_____
_____
_____
_____
_____
_____
_____

Mission Accomplished!   Date: _____

Fill out any thoughts here after you hit the spot (Ex: overall impression, how many photos you took, what you would do differently next time, memory to remember the trip by, best/worst thing that happened, etc.):

_____
_____
_____
_____
_____
_____
_____
_____
_____
_____
_____
_____
_____
_____
_____
_____
_____
_____
_____
_____
_____
_____

Shot Spot: _____

Date: _____

Distance: _____

Coordinates: _____

Address:
_____
_____

Email: _____

Website: _____

Time of Day: _____

Lighting (sunlight, flash, diffused light, etc.):
_____
_____

Gear List:
_____
_____
_____
_____

Fee? Yes or No/Amount$: _____

Need Permission? Yes or No/Notes:
_____
_____
_____
_____

Shot Spot Concept (What, how, etc.):

_____
_____
_____
_____
_____
_____
_____
_____
_____
_____
_____
_____
_____
_____

Sketch Area:

Tips from others who have been there (Google, friends):

_____
_____
_____
_____
_____
_____
_____
_____

Planning/Resources (Ex: social media pages, books to read, how many days, best month to go, book hotel, etc):

_____
_____
_____
_____
_____
_____
_____
_____
_____
_____
_____
_____
_____

Mission Accomplished! Date: _____

Fill out any thoughts here after you hit the spot (Ex: overall impression, how many photos you took, what you would do differently next time, memory to remember the trip by, best/worst thing that happened, etc.):

_____
_____
_____
_____
_____
_____
_____
_____
_____
_____
_____
_____
_____
_____
_____
_____
_____
_____
_____

Shot Spot: _____

Date: _____

Distance: _____

Coordinates: _____

Address:

_____

_____

Email: _____

Website: _____

Time of Day: _____

Lighting (sunlight, flash, diffused light, etc.):

_____

_____

Gear List:

_____

_____

_____

_____

Fee? Yes or No/Amount$: _____

Need Permission? Yes or No/Notes:

_____

_____

_____

_____

Shot Spot Concept (What, how, etc.):

_____
_____
_____
_____
_____
_____
_____
_____
_____
_____
_____
_____

Sketch Area:

Tips from others who have been there (Google, friends):

_____
_____
_____
_____
_____
_____
_____
_____
_____

Planning/Resources (Ex: social media pages, books to read, how many days, best month to go, book hotel, etc):

_____
_____
_____
_____
_____
_____
_____
_____
_____
_____
_____
_____

Mission Accomplished! Date: _____

Fill out any thoughts here after you hit the spot (Ex: overall impression, how many photos you took, what you would do differently next time, memory to remember the trip by, best/worst thing that happened, etc.):

_____
_____
_____
_____
_____
_____
_____
_____
_____
_____
_____
_____
_____
_____
_____
_____
_____
_____
_____
_____
_____

Shot Spot:_____

Date: _____

Distance: _____

Coordinates: _____

Address:
_____
_____

Email: _____

Website: _____

Time of Day: _____

Lighting (sunlight, flash, diffused light, etc.):
_____
_____

Gear List:
_____
_____
_____
_____

Fee? Yes or No/Amount$: _____

Need Permission? Yes or No/Notes:
_____
_____
_____
_____

Shot Spot Concept (What, how, etc.):

_____
_____
_____
_____
_____
_____
_____
_____
_____
_____
_____
_____

Sketch Area:

> *"Your photography is a record of your living, for anyone who really sees."* –Paul Strand

Tips from others who have been there (Google, friends, where to stay, where to eat):

_____
_____
_____
_____
_____
_____
_____
_____

Planning/Resources (Ex: social media pages, books to read, how many days, best month to go, book hotel, etc): _____
_____
_____
_____
_____
_____
_____
_____
_____

Mission Accomplished!   Date: _____

Fill out any thoughts here after you hit the spot (Ex: overall impression, how many photos you took, what you would do differently next time, memory to remember the trip by, best/worst thing that happened, etc.):

_____
_____
_____
_____
_____
_____
_____
_____
_____
_____
_____
_____
_____
_____
_____
_____
_____
_____
_____
_____
_____
_____

Shot Spot: _____

Date: _____

Distance: _____

Coordinates: _____

Address:

_____

_____

Email: _____

Website: _____

Time of Day: _____

Lighting (sunlight, flash, diffused light, etc.):

_____

_____

Gear List:

_____

_____

_____

_____

Fee? Yes or No/Amount$: _____

Need Permission? Yes or No/Notes:

_____

_____

_____

Shot Spot Concept (What, how, etc.):

_____
_____
_____
_____
_____
_____
_____
_____
_____
_____
_____
_____

Sketch Area:

Tips from others who have been there (Google, friends):

_____
_____
_____
_____
_____
_____
_____
_____

Planning/Resources (Ex: social media pages, books to read, how many days, best month to go, book hotel, etc):

_____
_____
_____
_____
_____
_____
_____
_____
_____
_____
_____
_____

Mission Accomplished! Date: _____

Fill out any thoughts here after you hit the spot (Ex: overall impression, how many photos you took, what you would do differently next time, memory to remember the trip by, best/worst thing that happened, etc.):

_____
_____
_____
_____
_____
_____
_____
_____
_____
_____
_____
_____
_____
_____
_____
_____
_____
_____
_____
_____

Shot Spot: _____

Date: _____

Distance: _____

Coordinates: _____

Address:
_____
_____

Email: _____

Website: _____

Time of Day: _____

Lighting (sunlight, flash, diffused light, etc.):
_____
_____

Gear List:
_____
_____
_____
_____

Fee? Yes or No/Amount$: _____

Need Permission? Yes or No/Notes:
_____
_____
_____
_____

Shot Spot Concept (What, how, etc.):

Sketch Area:

Tips from others who have been there (Google, friends):

_____
_____
_____
_____
_____
_____
_____
_____

Planning/Resources (Ex: social media pages, books to read, how many days, best month to go, book hotel, etc):

_____
_____
_____
_____
_____
_____
_____
_____
_____
_____
_____
_____

Mission Accomplished! Date: _____

Fill out any thoughts here after you hit the spot (Ex: overall impression, how many photos you took, what you would do differently next time, memory to remember the trip by, best/worst thing that happened, etc.):

_____
_____
_____
_____
_____
_____
_____
_____
_____
_____
_____
_____
_____
_____
_____
_____
_____
_____
_____
_____

Shot Spot: _____

Date: _____

Distance: _____

Coordinates: _____

Address:
_____
_____

Email: _____

Website: _____

Time of Day: _____

Lighting (sunlight, flash, diffused light, etc.):
_____
_____

Gear List:
_____
_____
_____
_____

Fee? Yes or No/Amount$: _____

Need Permission? Yes or No/Notes:
_____
_____
_____
_____

Shot Spot Concept (What, how, etc.):

Sketch Area:

Tips from others who have been there (Google, friends):

_____
_____
_____
_____
_____
_____
_____
_____
_____

Planning/Resources (Ex: social media pages, books to read, how many days, best month to go, book hotel, etc):

_____
_____
_____
_____
_____
_____
_____
_____
_____
_____
_____
_____

Mission Accomplished! Date: _____

Fill out any thoughts here after you hit the spot (Ex: overall impression, how many photos you took, what you would do differently next time, memory to remember the trip by, best/worst thing that happened, etc.):

_____
_____
_____
_____
_____
_____
_____
_____
_____
_____
_____
_____
_____
_____
_____
_____
_____
_____
_____
_____

Shot Spot: _____

Date: _____

Distance: _____

Coordinates: _____

Address:
_____
_____

Email: _____

Website: _____

Time of Day: _____

Lighting (sunlight, flash, diffused light, etc.):
_____
_____

Gear List:
_____
_____
_____
_____

Fee? Yes or No/Amount$: _____

Need Permission? Yes or No/Notes:
_____
_____
_____
_____

Shot Spot Concept (What, how, etc.):

Sketch Area:

> *"Landscape photography is the supreme test of the photographer - and often the supreme disappointment."*
> —Ansel Adams

Tips from others who have been there (Google, friends, where to stay, where to eat):

_____
_____
_____
_____
_____
_____
_____
_____

Planning/Resources (Ex: social media pages, books to read, how many days, best month to go, book hotel, etc): _____

_____
_____
_____
_____
_____
_____
_____
_____

Mission Accomplished! Date: _____

Fill out any thoughts here after you hit the spot (Ex: overall impression, how many photos you took, what you would do differently next time, memory to remember the trip by, best/worst thing that happened, etc.):

_____
_____
_____
_____
_____
_____
_____
_____
_____
_____
_____
_____
_____
_____
_____
_____
_____
_____
_____
_____

Shot Spot: _____

Date: _____

Distance: _____

Coordinates: _____

Address:
_____
_____

Email: _____

Website: _____

Time of Day: _____

Lighting (sunlight, flash, diffused light, etc.):
_____
_____

Gear List:
_____
_____
_____
_____

Fee? Yes or No/Amount$: _____

Need Permission? Yes or No/Notes:
_____
_____
_____
_____

Shot Spot Concept (What, how, etc.):

Sketch Area:

Tips from others who have been there (Google, friends):

_____
_____
_____
_____
_____
_____
_____
_____

Planning/Resources (Ex: social media pages, books to read, how many days, best month to go, book hotel, etc):

_____
_____
_____
_____
_____
_____
_____
_____
_____
_____
_____
_____

Mission Accomplished! Date: _____

Fill out any thoughts here after you hit the spot (Ex: overall impression, how many photos you took, what you would do differently next time, memory to remember the trip by, best/worst thing that happened, etc.):

_____
_____
_____
_____
_____
_____
_____
_____
_____
_____
_____
_____
_____
_____
_____
_____
_____
_____
_____
_____

Shot Spot: _____

Date: _____

Distance: _____

Coordinates: _____

Address:
_____
_____

Email: _____

Website: _____

Time of Day: _____

Lighting (sunlight, flash, diffused light, etc.):
_____
_____

Gear List:
_____
_____
_____
_____

Fee? Yes or No/Amount$: _____

Need Permission? Yes or No/Notes:
_____
_____
_____
_____

Shot Spot Concept (What, how, etc.):

Sketch Area:

Tips from others who have been there (Google, friends):

_____
_____
_____
_____
_____
_____
_____
_____

Planning/Resources (Ex: social media pages, books to read, how many days, best month to go, book hotel, etc):

_____
_____
_____
_____
_____
_____
_____
_____
_____
_____
_____
_____

Mission Accomplished! Date: _____

Fill out any thoughts here after you hit the spot (Ex: overall impression, how many photos you took, what you would do differently next time, memory to remember the trip by, best/worst thing that happened, etc.):

_____
_____
_____
_____
_____
_____
_____
_____
_____
_____
_____
_____
_____
_____
_____
_____
_____
_____
_____
_____

Shot Spot: _____

Date: _____

Distance: _____

Coordinates: _____

Address:
_____
_____

Email: _____

Website: _____

Time of Day: _____

Lighting (sunlight, flash, diffused light, etc.):
_____
_____

Gear List:
_____
_____
_____
_____

Fee? Yes or No/Amount$: _____

Need Permission? Yes or No/Notes:
_____
_____
_____
_____

Shot Spot Concept (What, how, etc.):

_____
_____
_____
_____
_____
_____
_____
_____
_____
_____
_____
_____
_____

Sketch Area:

Tips from others who have been there (Google, friends):

_____
_____
_____
_____
_____
_____
_____
_____

Planning/Resources (Ex: social media pages, books to read, how many days, best month to go, book hotel, etc):

_____
_____
_____
_____
_____
_____
_____
_____
_____
_____
_____
_____

Mission Accomplished! Date: _____

Fill out any thoughts here after you hit the spot (Ex: overall impression, how many photos you took, what you would do differently next time, memory to remember the trip by, best/worst thing that happened, etc.):

_____
_____
_____
_____
_____
_____
_____
_____
_____
_____
_____
_____
_____
_____
_____
_____
_____
_____
_____
_____

Shot Spot: _____

Date: _____

Distance: _____

Coordinates: _____

Address:
_____
_____

Email: _____

Website: _____

Time of Day: _____

Lighting (sunlight, flash, diffused light, etc.):
_____
_____

Gear List:
_____
_____
_____
_____

Fee? Yes or No/Amount$: _____

Need Permission? Yes or No/Notes:
_____
_____
_____
_____

Shot Spot Concept (What, how, etc.):

Sketch Area:

"In a world and a life that moves so fast, photography just makes the sound go out and it makes you stop and take a pause. Photography calms me." -Drew Barrymore

Tips from others who have been there (Google, friends, where to stay, where to eat):

_____
_____
_____
_____
_____
_____
_____
_____

Planning/Resources (Ex: social media pages, books to read, how many days, best month to go, book hotel, etc): _____

_____
_____
_____
_____
_____
_____
_____
_____

Mission Accomplished!   Date: _____

Fill out any thoughts here after you hit the spot (Ex: overall impression, how many photos you took, what you would do differently next time, memory to remember the trip by, best/worst thing that happened, etc.):

_____
_____
_____
_____
_____
_____
_____
_____
_____
_____
_____
_____
_____
_____
_____
_____
_____
_____
_____

Shot Spot: _____

Date: _____

Distance: _____

Coordinates: _____

Address:
_____
_____

Email: _____

Website: _____

Time of Day: _____

Lighting (sunlight, flash, diffused light, etc.):
_____
_____

Gear List:
_____
_____
_____
_____

Fee? Yes or No/Amount$: _____

Need Permission? Yes or No/Notes:
_____
_____
_____
_____

Shot Spot Concept (What, how, etc.):

Sketch Area:

Tips from others who have been there (Google, friends):

_____
_____
_____
_____
_____
_____
_____
_____

Planning/Resources (Ex: social media pages, books to read, how many days, best month to go, book hotel, etc):

_____
_____
_____
_____
_____
_____
_____
_____
_____
_____
_____

Mission Accomplished! Date: _____

Fill out any thoughts here after you hit the spot (Ex: overall impression, how many photos you took, what you would do differently next time, memory to remember the trip by, best/worst thing that happened, etc.):

_____
_____
_____
_____
_____
_____
_____
_____
_____
_____
_____
_____
_____
_____
_____
_____
_____
_____
_____

Shot Spot: _____

Date: _____

Distance: _____

Coordinates: _____

Address:
_____
_____

Email: _____

Website: _____

Time of Day: _____

Lighting (sunlight, flash, diffused light, etc.):
_____
_____

Gear List:
_____
_____
_____
_____

Fee? Yes or No/Amount$: _____

Need Permission? Yes or No/Notes:
_____
_____
_____
_____

Shot Spot Concept (What, how, etc.):

Sketch Area:

Tips from others who have been there (Google, friends):

_____
_____
_____
_____
_____
_____
_____
_____

Planning/Resources (Ex: social media pages, books to read, how many days, best month to go, book hotel, etc):

_____
_____
_____
_____
_____
_____
_____
_____
_____
_____
_____
_____

Mission Accomplished!   Date: _____

Fill out any thoughts here after you hit the spot (Ex: overall impression, how many photos you took, what you would do differently next time, memory to remember the trip by, best/worst thing that happened, etc.):

_____
_____
_____
_____
_____
_____
_____
_____
_____
_____
_____
_____
_____
_____
_____
_____
_____
_____
_____
_____
_____
_____
_____

Shot Spot: _____

Date: _____

Distance: _____

Coordinates: _____

Address:
_____
_____

Email: _____

Website: _____

Time of Day: _____

Lighting (sunlight, flash, diffused light, etc.):
_____
_____

Gear List:
_____
_____
_____
_____

Fee? Yes or No/Amount$: _____

Need Permission? Yes or No/Notes:
_____
_____
_____
_____

Shot Spot Concept (What, how, etc.):

Sketch Area:

Tips from others who have been there (Google, friends):

_____
_____
_____
_____
_____
_____
_____
_____

Planning/Resources (Ex: social media pages, books to read, how many days, best month to go, book hotel, etc):

_____
_____
_____
_____
_____
_____
_____
_____
_____
_____
_____

Mission Accomplished! Date: _____

Fill out any thoughts here after you hit the spot (Ex: overall impression, how many photos you took, what you would do differently next time, memory to remember the trip by, best/worst thing that happened, etc.):

_____
_____
_____
_____
_____
_____
_____
_____
_____
_____
_____
_____
_____
_____
_____
_____
_____
_____
_____
_____

Shot Spot: _____

Date: _____

Distance: _____

Coordinates: _____

Address:
_____
_____

Email: _____

Website: _____

Time of Day: _____

Lighting (sunlight, flash, diffused light, etc.):
_____
_____

Gear List:
_____
_____
_____
_____

Fee? Yes or No/Amount$: _____

Need Permission? Yes or No/Notes:
_____
_____
_____
_____

Shot Spot Concept (What, how, etc.):

Sketch Area:

> "Black and white are the colors of photography. To me they symbolize the alternatives of hope and despair to which mankind is forever subjected." -Robert Frank

Tips from others who have been there (Google, friends, where to stay, where to eat):

_____
_____
_____
_____
_____
_____
_____
_____

Planning/Resources (Ex: social media pages, books to read, how many days, best month to go, book hotel, etc): _____

_____
_____
_____
_____
_____
_____
_____

Mission Accomplished! Date: _____

Fill out any thoughts here after you hit the spot (Ex: overall impression, how many photos you took, what you would do differently next time, memory to remember the trip by, best/worst thing that happened, etc.):

_____
_____
_____
_____
_____
_____
_____
_____
_____
_____
_____
_____
_____
_____
_____
_____
_____
_____
_____
_____

Shot Spot: _____

Date: _____

Distance: _____

Coordinates: _____

Address:
_____
_____

Email: _____

Website: _____

Time of Day: _____

Lighting (sunlight, flash, diffused light, etc.):
_____
_____

Gear List:
_____
_____
_____
_____

Fee? Yes or No/Amount$: _____

Need Permission? Yes or No/Notes:
_____
_____
_____
_____

Shot Spot Concept (What, how, etc.):

_____
_____
_____
_____
_____
_____
_____
_____
_____
_____
_____
_____
_____

Sketch Area:

Tips from others who have been there (Google, friends):

_____
_____
_____
_____
_____
_____
_____
_____

Planning/Resources (Ex: social media pages, books to read, how many days, best month to go, book hotel, etc):

_____
_____
_____
_____
_____
_____
_____
_____
_____
_____
_____
_____

Mission Accomplished! Date: _____

Fill out any thoughts here after you hit the spot (Ex: overall impression, how many photos you took, what you would do differently next time, memory to remember the trip by, best/worst thing that happened, etc.):

_____
_____
_____
_____
_____
_____
_____
_____
_____
_____
_____
_____
_____
_____
_____
_____
_____
_____
_____
_____

Shot Spot: _____

Date: _____

Distance: _____

Coordinates: _____

Address:
_____
_____

Email: _____

Website: _____

Time of Day: _____

Lighting (sunlight, flash, diffused light, etc.):
_____
_____

Gear List:
_____
_____
_____
_____

Fee? Yes or No/Amount$: _____

Need Permission? Yes or No/Notes:
_____
_____
_____
_____

Shot Spot Concept (What, how, etc.):

Sketch Area:

Tips from others who have been there (Google, friends):

_____
_____
_____
_____
_____
_____
_____
_____

Planning/Resources (Ex: social media pages, books to read, how many days, best month to go, book hotel, etc):

_____
_____
_____
_____
_____
_____
_____
_____
_____
_____
_____
_____

Mission Accomplished! Date: _____

Fill out any thoughts here after you hit the spot (Ex: overall impression, how many photos you took, what you would do differently next time, memory to remember the trip by, best/worst thing that happened, etc.):

_____
_____
_____
_____
_____
_____
_____
_____
_____
_____
_____
_____
_____
_____
_____
_____
_____
_____
_____

Shot Spot: _____

Date: _____

Distance: _____

Coordinates: _____

Address:

_____

_____

Email: _____

Website: _____

Time of Day: _____

Lighting (sunlight, flash, diffused light, etc.):

_____

_____

Gear List:

_____

_____

_____

_____

Fee? Yes or No/Amount$: _____

Need Permission? Yes or No/Notes:

_____

_____

_____

_____

Shot Spot Concept (What, how, etc.):

Sketch Area:

Tips from others who have been there (Google, friends):
_____
_____
_____
_____
_____
_____
_____
_____

Planning/Resources (Ex: social media pages, books to read, how many days, best month to go, book hotel, etc):
_____
_____
_____
_____
_____
_____
_____
_____
_____
_____
_____
_____

Mission Accomplished! Date: _____

Fill out any thoughts here after you hit the spot (Ex: overall impression, how many photos you took, what you would do differently next time, memory to remember the trip by, best/worst thing that happened, etc.):

_____
_____
_____
_____
_____
_____
_____
_____
_____
_____
_____
_____
_____
_____
_____
_____
_____
_____
_____
_____

Shot Spot: _____

Date: _____

Distance: _____

Coordinates: _____

Address:
_____
_____

Email: _____

Website: _____

Time of Day: _____

Lighting (sunlight, flash, diffused light, etc.):
_____
_____

Gear List:
_____
_____
_____
_____

Fee? Yes or No/Amount$: _____

Need Permission? Yes or No/Notes:
_____
_____
_____
_____

Shot Spot Concept (What, how, etc.):

_____
_____
_____
_____
_____
_____
_____
_____
_____
_____
_____

Sketch Area:

> "One advantage of photography is that it's visual and can transcend language." —Lisa Kristine

Tips from others who have been there (Google, friends, where to stay, where to eat):

_____
_____
_____
_____
_____
_____
_____
_____

Planning/Resources (Ex: social media pages, books to read, how many days, best month to go, book hotel, etc): _____

_____
_____
_____
_____
_____
_____
_____
_____
_____

Mission Accomplished! Date: _____

Fill out any thoughts here after you hit the spot (Ex: overall impression, how many photos you took, what you would do differently next time, memory to remember the trip by, best/worst thing that happened, etc.):

_____
_____
_____
_____
_____
_____
_____
_____
_____
_____
_____
_____
_____
_____
_____
_____
_____
_____
_____
_____
_____

Shot Spot: _____

Date: _____

Distance: _____

Coordinates: _____

Address:

_____

_____

Email: _____

Website: _____

Time of Day: _____

Lighting (sunlight, flash, diffused light, etc.):

_____

_____

Gear List:

_____

_____

_____

_____

Fee? Yes or No/Amount$: _____

Need Permission? Yes or No/Notes:

_____

_____

_____

_____

Shot Spot Concept (What, how, etc.):

Sketch Area:

Tips from others who have been there (Google, friends):
_____
_____
_____
_____
_____
_____
_____
_____

Planning/Resources (Ex: social media pages, books to read, how many days, best month to go, book hotel, etc):
_____
_____
_____
_____
_____
_____
_____
_____
_____
_____
_____
_____
_____

Mission Accomplished! Date: _____

Fill out any thoughts here after you hit the spot (Ex: overall impression, how many photos you took, what you would do differently next time, memory to remember the trip by, best/worst thing that happened, etc.):

_____
_____
_____
_____
_____
_____
_____
_____
_____
_____
_____
_____
_____
_____
_____
_____
_____
_____
_____
_____

Shot Spot:_____

Date: _____

Distance: _____

Coordinates: _____

Address:
_____
_____

Email: _____

Website: _____

Time of Day: _____

Lighting (sunlight, flash, diffused light, etc.):
_____
_____

Gear List:
_____
_____
_____
_____

Fee? Yes or No/Amount$: _____

Need Permission? Yes or No/Notes:
_____
_____
_____

Shot Spot Concept (What, how, etc.):

_____
_____
_____
_____
_____
_____
_____
_____
_____
_____
_____

Sketch Area:

Tips from others who have been there (Google, friends):

_____
_____
_____
_____
_____
_____
_____
_____

Planning/Resources (Ex: social media pages, books to read, how many days, best month to go, book hotel, etc):

_____
_____
_____
_____
_____
_____
_____
_____
_____
_____
_____
_____

Mission Accomplished! Date: _____

Fill out any thoughts here after you hit the spot (Ex: overall impression, how many photos you took, what you would do differently next time, memory to remember the trip by, best/worst thing that happened, etc.):

_____
_____
_____
_____
_____
_____
_____
_____
_____
_____
_____
_____
_____
_____
_____
_____
_____
_____
_____
_____

Shot Spot: _____

Date: _____

Distance: _____

Coordinates: _____

Address:
_____
_____

Email: _____

Website: _____

Time of Day: _____

Lighting (sunlight, flash, diffused light, etc.):
_____
_____

Gear List:
_____
_____
_____
_____

Fee? Yes or No/Amount$: _____

Need Permission? Yes or No/Notes:
_____
_____
_____
_____

Shot Spot Concept (What, how, etc.):

Sketch Area:

Tips from others who have been there (Google, friends):

_____
_____
_____
_____
_____
_____
_____
_____

Planning/Resources (Ex: social media pages, books to read, how many days, best month to go, book hotel, etc):

_____
_____
_____
_____
_____
_____
_____
_____
_____
_____
_____
_____

Mission Accomplished! Date: _____

Fill out any thoughts here after you hit the spot (Ex: overall impression, how many photos you took, what you would do differently next time, memory to remember the trip by, best/worst thing that happened, etc.):

Shot Spot: _____

Date: _____

Distance: _____

Coordinates: _____

Address:

_____

_____

Email: _____

Website: _____

Time of Day: _____

Lighting (sunlight, flash, diffused light, etc.):

_____

_____

Gear List:

_____

_____

_____

_____

Fee? Yes or No/Amount$: _____

Need Permission? Yes or No/Notes:

_____

_____

_____

_____

Shot Spot Concept (What, how, etc.):

Sketch Area:

> "I really believe in challenging myself, pushing myself to new places." —Jonathan Evison

Tips from others who have been there (Google, friends, where to stay, where to eat):

_____
_____
_____
_____
_____
_____
_____

Planning/Resources (Ex: social media pages, books to read, how many days, best month to go, book hotel, etc): _____

_____
_____
_____
_____
_____
_____
_____

Mission Accomplished!   Date: _____

Fill out any thoughts here after you hit the spot (Ex: overall impression, how many photos you took, what you would do differently next time, memory to remember the trip by, best/worst thing that happened, etc.):

_____
_____
_____
_____
_____
_____
_____
_____
_____
_____
_____
_____
_____
_____
_____
_____
_____
_____
_____
_____

Shot Spot: _____

Date: _____

Distance: _____

Coordinates: _____

Address:
_____
_____

Email: _____

Website: _____

Time of Day: _____

Lighting (sunlight, flash, diffused light, etc.):
_____
_____

Gear List:
_____
_____
_____
_____

Fee? Yes or No/Amount$: _____

Need Permission? Yes or No/Notes:
_____
_____
_____
_____

Shot Spot Concept (What, how, etc.):

Sketch Area:

Tips from others who have been there (Google, friends):

_____
_____
_____
_____
_____
_____
_____
_____

Planning/Resources (Ex: social media pages, books to read, how many days, best month to go, book hotel, etc):

_____
_____
_____
_____
_____
_____
_____
_____
_____
_____
_____
_____

Mission Accomplished! Date: _____

Fill out any thoughts here after you hit the spot (Ex: overall impression, how many photos you took, what you would do differently next time, memory to remember the trip by, best/worst thing that happened, etc.):

_____
_____
_____
_____
_____
_____
_____
_____
_____
_____
_____
_____
_____
_____
_____
_____
_____
_____
_____
_____

Shot Spot: _____

Date: _____

Distance: _____

Coordinates: _____

Address:
_____
_____

Email: _____

Website: _____

Time of Day: _____

Lighting (sunlight, flash, diffused light, etc.):
_____
_____

Gear List:
_____
_____
_____
_____

Fee? Yes or No/Amount$: _____

Need Permission? Yes or No/Notes:
_____
_____
_____
_____

Shot Spot Concept (What, how, etc.):

Sketch Area:

Tips from others who have been there (Google, friends):
_____
_____
_____
_____
_____
_____
_____
_____

Planning/Resources (Ex: social media pages, books to read, how many days, best month to go, book hotel, etc):
_____
_____
_____
_____
_____
_____
_____
_____
_____
_____
_____
_____

Mission Accomplished! Date: _____

Fill out any thoughts here after you hit the spot (Ex: overall impression, how many photos you took, what you would do differently next time, memory to remember the trip by, best/worst thing that happened, etc.):

_____
_____
_____
_____
_____
_____
_____
_____
_____
_____
_____
_____
_____
_____
_____
_____
_____
_____

Shot Spot:_____

Date: _____

Distance: _____

Coordinates: _____

Address:
_____
_____

Email: _____

Website: _____

Time of Day: _____

Lighting (sunlight, flash, diffused light, etc.):
_____
_____

Gear List:
_____
_____
_____
_____

Fee? Yes or No/Amount$: _____

Need Permission? Yes or No/Notes:
_____
_____
_____
_____

Shot Spot Concept (What, how, etc.):

Sketch Area:

> "Photography is more than a medium for factual communication of ideas. It is a creative art."
> -Ansel Adams

Tips from others who have been there (Google, friends, where to stay, where to eat):

_____
_____
_____
_____
_____
_____
_____
_____

Planning/Resources (Ex: social media pages, books to read, how many days, best month to go, book hotel, etc): _____

_____
_____
_____
_____
_____
_____
_____
_____

Mission Accomplished!   Date: _____

Fill out any thoughts here after you hit the spot (Ex: overall impression, how many photos you took, what you would do differently next time, memory to remember the trip by, best/worst thing that happened, etc.):

_____
_____
_____
_____
_____
_____
_____
_____
_____
_____
_____
_____
_____
_____
_____
_____
_____
_____
_____
_____
_____
_____

Thank you for buying this book! It is my hope that you found it very useful. I actually created it so I could have one! I plan on publishing other photography & non-photography related journals soon.

I have one resource for you to get started planning new shot spots: *www.roadtrippers.com*

If you would like to check out some of my photography - remember, I am a work in progress!

My Facebook page is: *www.facebook.com/sunlionimagery*

My flickr page is: *www.flickr.com/photos/sunlionimagery*

                                                  Best wishes,
                                                  Barbara Jean

CPSIA information can be obtained at www.ICGtesting.com
Printed in the USA
BVOW09s2330041215

429416BV00013B/161/P